FORGIVENESS THROUGH THE EYES OF MY REFLECTION

BY

CORINNA TACKETT

This book reflects the author's present recollections of experiences over time. Some names and identifying characteristics have been changed to respect those individuals' privacy.

FOREWORD

Let me introduce you to a warrior. Corinna and I became friends years ago when we were both on the prayer team at church. While the prayer team's main objective was always praying for the Pastor, the service, and the people, eventually each person had one of those days that they just laid their hearts out before the other team members.

I remember the first time she spoke about her life, and I thought, "I've had struggles, but this lady has been through some stuff. How could someone who has been through so much be so full of love for others? How in the world can she forgive? I know we should, but I mean, some things are just too unforgivable, right?"

Not according to God, and not according to Corinna. Over and over, as the days, weeks and years went by, I heard and saw her love for people. She is full of compassion in situations where I thought, "Nope, no way, not me." She is a genuine, down-to-earth person who consistently loves God, her family, and others. She is someone who has been to hell and back more than once, yet forgiveness and compassion are her anchors. I've watched her live out her message and His message daily. I am

2

blessed to call her my friend, and I encourage you to not only read the story of her life, but allow it to open your heart to courage, to hope, to forgiveness, to restoration, and ultimately, to God.

~ Kevin Cruise, prayer team member, Granite City Church

PREFACE

Brrring, brrring.

I answered the phone quickly.

"This is Harry with Census 2000," spoke a deep voice on the other end. "I need to confirm an address for this phone number as we are doing an update."

I responded, "The address you have is incorrect," and promptly gave him the correction. Census 2000 was a mandatory count of the population since Y2K, so I thought nothing of it. Our conversation was pleasant, and I hung up the phone and proceeded to rest a little more before my mom and step dad got home.

Brrring, brrring

Who is calling now? I thought.

"Hello, yes, Corinna?" The deep voice sounded familiar from just a few moments prior. "Yes, this is she"—

I couldn't even finish my sentence, because of a sudden banging on my front door.

"U.S. Marshals. Come to the front door!" Harry was no census worker; I had instead told the US Marshals where to find me.

My ears began to ring and my heart pounded as I walked to the front door and opened it to a world unknown to me. Men and women with bulletproof vests were in the front yard. Guns pointed at me as I opened the door and stepped out. Down to the ground I went.

"Ms. Holland, you have the right to remain silent. Anything you say can and will be used against you in a court of law. You have the right to have an attorney. If you cannot afford an attorney, one will be provided for you."

This is my story.

CHAPTER ONE
Built on a Faulty Foundation

I had been in and out of every school you could imagine. My mom had been married numerous times, all of which seemed like epic fails. I could not make friends or get attached to my favorite toys because they would be left when my mom decided we were running to the next county or state. Moments as a child were so scattered. I had never met my biological father, and a father figure was non-existent in my life for the most part.

My brother and I had two half-brothers named Duane and Marty from Mom's first marriage. We would see them on holidays or birthdays. They chose to live with their dad when my mom divorced him. My baby brother and I were from one of her relationships a few years later. Seeing them on special occasions was a part of life to which we had grown accustomed. Marty and Duane were special playmates that we got to see when holidays rolled around.

My mom gave birth to my baby brother Dickie in 1973 and ten months later, she gave birth to me. Many years later, when Dickie and I were old enough to understand, she explained that our father had left her for another woman. When we were a little older than that, she explained further that he was married to another woman while she was in a relationship with him. I was a little shocked, but also annoyed. Sure, I felt bad that she had been left and cheated on. But shouldn't she have known that playing around with a married man would end up badly?

Years later, my mom introduced my brother and me to another older man. "Kids, I would like for you to meet Bill." He was white-headed and looked to be several years older than my mom. He walked staggered as he had a brace on one shoe with the sole built up to it. His voice was raspy and profound, and I assume it was from several years of smoking. He had a cowgirl tattooed on his upper arm, which was faded and must have been done in his younger days.

As a kid, I wasn't quite sure what each new relationship would entail. Bill was kind to my brother and me. In time, we would realize he was strict, but at the same time, we saw that he was going to provide for us. If he called your name for you to come to him, he expected a, "Yes, sir."

After several months of Mama and Bill living together, they decided to get married. Mama asked Dickie and me if we wanted to have Bill's last name. I was thrilled that this guy wanted to adopt us. Indeed, he was going to be around for a time. I felt like we finally had a firm foundation after an ever-shifting life as kids. We both wholeheartedly agreed to take his last name. For me, it gave me a sense of belonging.

Teen years were approaching for me. The once-little girl was not so little anymore. Hormones had taken hold of me, and things were blossoming from every side of my body you could imagine. It seemed as though I jumped into wearing women's size bras and not the "trainees" that the other girls my age were wearing. At the age of ten, I became a young lady, so-to-speak. The preteen years are crazy for kids trying to adjust to everything their body is trying to throw at them, and it was no different for me.

My mom became a Tupperware consultant and held parties in the evenings. I think that she started doing this to make a little spending money and to get out of the house once in a while. Mom was now a housewife, which was a different element than in previous marriages. I think having a side job gave her a sense of fulfillment outside the home.

One evening while my mom was away, my dad called me into the living room and asked if I would boil his ears out with peroxide. Older guys like that seemed to lose the hair on top of their head and gain what they lost in their ears.

He laid down in my lap on the couch, head parallel outward at first for that ear and then inward towards me for the other. The stench of a red Marlboro rose up from his shirt. His breathing was heavy as if he had run a mile to get there. While his ear was making the bubbling sensation, out of nowhere he bit me on my breast.

I immediately jumped. "Ouch!" I exclaimed. Where did that come from, and why? I thought.

"Did I hurt you?" he said. A little speck of blood had come through my bra where he had bitten. Nothing else was mentioned about this moment. Fear crept inside immediately for I had seen a side to him that I did not like.

I took a cotton ball and placed it into the ear and wiggled it around to absorb the peroxide, and then went to my room. Something did not sit right with me about what happened. Why did Dad do that? Did I do something wrong? I was so uncomfortable around him by myself after that evening.

Every time mom left the house, he tried to back me into a corner in the hallway or ask me to kiss him. I was a scared little girl that had nowhere to run. For months I had thought about telling my mom what Bill was doing. Several times I tried to make excuses to go with my mom so that I did not have to stay there with him alone.

One day while mom was away, he asked me to come into the kitchen and sit at the table. His words pierced my ears as if I had just heard a gun go off. "You get that you're not my real daughter, right? If you say anything to anyone about me, there is nothing that they can do, get it? They would not believe you anyway."

I was empty and alone. As much as I hated to admit it, Bill was right. No one would believe the story that I would tell them. On the outside, he portrayed himself as an excellent man. He was a provider for us and had shown that in the years my mom was with him.

I put up with his games and secrets for what seemed like a lifetime.

And I felt so dirty.

I began to get into fights at school. Too many conflicts to count. I despised the world around me and was looking for a reason to take my anger out on anything—or anyone—I could get my hands on. The school I went to was challenging. Kids bullied and picked on me. I would come out of the situation swinging, and it did not matter how petty the argument or picking was. I wanted to fight and prove myself to anyone that enjoyed the challenge.

They knew my mom on a first-name basis; she had come to pick me up several times for fighting. She could walk into the school's front door, and they would immediately respond with, "Yes, Mrs. Holland, Corinna is waiting in the principal's office for you; please go right back."

I had made friends with a hippie chick from high school. She had a carefree spirit and did not care what people thought of her. She would pick my brother and me up in the mornings and take us to school occasionally. Sometimes we would attend school, and other days we would skip; it depended on how we felt that morning. She would light up a joint and pass it around, and with her, that was my first time smoking marijuana. I enjoyed it because it seemed to take the edge off my anxiety and my secret. When I was high, I didn't think about dirtiness. I didn't dwell on the turmoil at home. The downside was that I could not feel that way all the time. My mom would catch on if I made it plain that I was stoned. The minute I came back down from the high, the bad feelings were still there, and I was just as empty as before I got high. More and more, I wanted to tell mom what was going on. My thoughts were endless as to how I would approach her.

CHAPTER TWO

Hodgepodge

One day Bill had gone outside to bush hog our land. We had several acres, and I knew it would take a while. He would spend at least half a day out there before stopping.

"Mama, can I talk to you?" I asked timidly, my stomach in knots.

"Of course," she said.

"I need to tell you something, and I don't want you to get mad at me." There was a lump in my throat the size of Texas, for this would not be easy for me. "Dad has been messing with me, not in a daughter way. Every time you leave, Mama, he tries to kiss me or touch me."

Her response came quickly, and it was what Bill had said it would be. "Did you sleep with him? If you did, so help me God, I'll kill you!"

Her words were like none I had ever heard. She spoke to me as if I was another woman enjoying what he had been trying to do. I was twelve and still playing with Barbie dolls! I was not trying to be the other woman. I got nauseous whenever I thought he would touch or mess with me. She did not believe me. She thought I was trying to cause turmoil in the home.

What about me? I thought. I didn't know how much longer I could put up with the games he played while she was away.

We stayed there with him several months longer. Every day was too long. They treated me like I was a total outcast for a while. I didn't care anymore. Anything that I had confidence in or had trusted had been demolished.

CHAPTER THREE

No Place to Land

Months later, I was cleaning my room, and mom came to the doorway. Of course, cleaning for me was stuffing all my clothes into the drawers and shoving stuff under the bed.

"I am gonna take a soaking bath," she announced.

"Ok, Mama," I replied.

When I got done cleaning, I noticed that Mama had been in her bath for a long time. Something seemed off to me, and I needed to check on her. I immediately went to her bedroom door and realized Mama had locked it. I grabbed a stool from my room and pulled it to the door to get one of our emergency keys on the top of the door frame in case we locked it accidentally. I opened the door and walked into the bathroom.

Mama was not there.

I turned to my left and saw a glimpse of Mama's legs lying on the floor between the wall and the bed. As I got closer, I saw that she had a gun in her hand and an open bottle of pills on the floor beside her.

"Mama!" I called, but no response came. I ran to dial 911.

After the paramedics got there, they asked me to step out. They had to work on her immediately. Standing outside the bedroom door, tiptoeing so I could see, they took a tube and fed her a black substance down her throat. She began to throw up. Shortly afterwards they took her away to the hospital.

My immediate emotions led to accusations in the mirror. Mama hurt herself because of me, I thought. I was the problem child. I was the one that told her what was going on behind the scenes, and it broke her heart. Why did I ever say anything at all? I should have just kept it to myself. All my life, I felt like things had happened to me because I was the guilty one. Always guilty.

After Mama got home from the hospital, things seemed different. We never discussed her episode again. We had all become very good at sweeping emotions under the rug. It didn't hurt as bad if you didn't talk about it. I was thankful to have her home and grateful she was still alive.

One day soon after, Mama called me from the kitchen. I could hear the urgency in her voice. "I need you to pack some clothes; we are leaving."

"Yes, ma'am," I replied. There was no extensive explanation at the moment, but I felt like she was carrying us away to the Promised Land. I had been ready to go months before this moment. I knew I was going with her, and the life before us had to be better than what I had been experiencing the last several months.

We stayed with some friends until we could get on our feet. In the years prior to Bill, my baby brother and I were used to moving "Johnny-on-the-spot." As I mentioned before, we knew at an early age not to get attached to things.

Mama explained that we were starting over and that she could not take my adopted father's mess anymore.

Why the sudden change? She had caught him in a lie. He had always given her the excuse that he was impotent and could not have sexual relations with her, but to her surprise, she found him masturbating one day in the bathroom. Bill was significantly older than her— more than twenty years—so it was not hard for her to believe that he couldn't perform husbandly duties, and this, in turn, was her reason for not believing me. Catching him in the act was my saving grace. I would not be molested by him anymore, and for me, this moment was a life raft.

Years and months came and went. To call it a downward spiral was an understatement. I gravitated to ones with more dysfunction than myself. Having friends like this helped me not feel so inadequate for what was going on in my own life. Being friends with misfits also felt comfortable. I didn't have to be questioned about why my life was a wreck. It just seemed to be a natural way of life for all those around me.

As a senior in high school, my relationship with my mom worsened. We could never see eye to eye on anything. We always ended up in fights, whether physical or verbal. My heart had been broken by people so many times, and I did not want this to happen again. I was not sure at the moment what I was expecting from her. All I knew was that I was tired of arguing and all the nonsense. I moved in with a friend over in the next town to us. We had agreed I could stay on her couch and I would pay for groceries. I intended to be out as soon as I saved some money to get into my own place. I would still attend school and wanted to graduate, even if it was by the skin of my teeth.

One night when I came home from work, my roommate had brought a guy home with her. She introduced him, and we partied and laughed all night. I had not had a good time like that in quite a while. Of course, at that age, I was always about having a good time. When the good times came, I didn't have to think of the bad times. The bad times tortured my mind constantly, knowing I was not what people thought I should be. The trauma of being molested and having an unstable childhood left me feeling hopeless and unworthy. Mom and my teachers all had expectations of me to be a better daughter, a better student, yet countless times I failed to meet that by getting into fights or skipping school.

Later that night, she and that guy went to her bedroom. Automatically I knew what would happen next, which was my roommate's business. I passed out on the couch with no care in the world. The numb feeling of being high would help me rest, and I knew that.

Hours later, I was awakened by that guy on top of me. He put his hand over my mouth to muffle the sound of me saying "No" and "don't." He forced himself on me. I tried to fight him, but I had no strength in my arms and legs, as they felt like jello. As soon as he was finished, he got up and went back to the bedroom. And there I lay crying, empty, and with yet another layer of dirt added to the pile of junk that had been placed on me at such a young age. I did not cry too loud, because my old wounds made me think that my roommate would have the crazy idea that I was after her man if she heard me and found out he raped me. After all, that is what had happened when I confronted Mama about Bill. It was like I was conditioned. Honestly, her thinking I sought out the sexual encounter was the last thing I wanted. It was better to stay silent in my torment.

As I was growing up, men always seemed to let me down or take advantage of me. Sadly, I learned this lesson from my mother. It was a lesson that I now knew very well.

A few weeks later, I headed to my oldest brother Duanes' house. He had been holding on to some clothes for me since I left my mom. That night I wanted to go to the bar and sing. Saturday nights were Karaoke nights at the bar. When I headed into the house, I knew immediately Duane had been drinking. He was never nice when he stepped across the threshold of 'too much'. He was mean and violent. I walked into his house and went upstairs to get my Caboodle—kind of like a fish and tackle box for makeup. Duane was angrily yelling at me, following me up the stairs.

"Where do you think you are going?" he asked.

"I am going to the bar," was my reply. "They're having Karaoke tonight, and I am going to sing."

Immediately, he became enraged. "You are going there to be a whore, aren't you?"

I would not let him talk to me like this. "I am eighteen, and I am going to do whatever I want, and you can't stop me!" When I turned around toward him, that Caboodle came right toward the side of my face.

I saw stars.

He hit me with it, and it was hard. I lost my balance at the top of the stairs and tumbled down. When I could breathe, I yelled, "You know what, Duane? You are just like your mama! I'm done with you both!" I stormed out and got into my car. I was going now, and no one was going to stop me.

CHAPTER FOUR
Breaking Point

The following day was a breaking point for me. I could hardly move. My back and legs were killing me. The adrenaline from the fight with my brother, Duane, had blocked the pain for the moment the night before, but it was being felt now. I told my roommate she would have to help me up. I knew I had something wrong with my back where I had fallen. She explained that because I was eighteen, I may be able to go to the local health department and that they have programs where someone would see me for my back pain.

Several weeks later, I was indeed seen at the Health Department. They asked several questions. They explained that through these services, to be seen or receive any medications, I had to have a pregnancy test to verify a negative result. I waited patiently in that room for what seemed like an eternity, and then a nurse came back into the room. "You're gonna need to apply for Medicaid today, sweetheart, while you are here. Your test is positive."

What? Are you serious?

I immediately began to cry. What was I going to do? The nurse asked if I knew who the father was, but I did not want to tell her what had happened. I couldn't give her more than a first name anyway. I was wrecked. The guy that took advantage of me in my roommates' apartment was the father of this baby inside of me.

I was consumed with anger at myself for getting high that night. I had said no to him, but to me, that was not enough. I had been weakened by the drugs. I thought that if I wasn't so messed up, I could have fought him harder. I believed that I could have made him stop if I hadn't smoked or drank.

And now this problem. Where could I go from here?

Could I abort this child inside of me? I thought long and hard about that. I even had the bartender at the bar where I sang tell me that she would loan me the money to "fix the problem" if I needed her to.

No matter what happened, I knew I was going to have to make up with mama. I left on such bad terms. So many times, we came at each other in rage, and yet all the while, I loved her, and I loved her strong. She made me so angry because of the things I had to experience growing up, yet the little girl inside me wanted my mom to hold me. I wanted my mom to tell me everything was going to be alright. If anyone knew how to raise kids without a man, it was her. She was the strongest woman I knew. When things came at her, she would quickly be able to devise a plan and come out on the other side of it.

It was time to make amends.

I sat mom down and told her I was pregnant. I also told her the same story that I did not know who the father was. I did not want Mama to know the truth for fear of her going to my friend's apartment and making a terrible scene.

Mom took it well. So much better than I thought she would. "We will get through this," she said. "I will help you. However I can." Our relationship through the years had been dysfunctional, but I would take help however it came. I needed her support through this. Raising us kids through the years a lot of times by herself, she knew I needed her now more than ever.

After graduation, I got a job at a local convenience store. With full-time pay, I saved as much as possible to get my apartment. Still pregnant with a belly growing daily, I could never take the bartender up on her offer to pay for an abortion. Even with feeling emotionally the lowest of my life, I had to give this baby inside of me a fighting chance.

CHAPTER FIVE
Clinch the Deal

A few years later, I would try a relationship with an older woman named Faye. She had a daughter, Nina, in her early twenties, a little younger than I was. Nina worked at a local strip club as a cocktail waitress. Within weeks of Faye and I dating, we found a house to rent and moved in together. Nina and I became close friends. We got along excellently and partied together often. She was beautiful and funny. She had long hair and olive skin. She loved having the attention of the room; whether cracking jokes or dancing, she was an easygoing person that you could care for quickly.

Faye was a tomboy. She had jail tattoos and wore short, spiked hair. She was tough as nails and had been through some rough times in her life, which showed in her nature. I found comfort in that. I knew that by being her girlfriend, no one would mess with me.

Through the years, everywhere I had turned, a man had hurt me. I wanted to give this lesbian relationship a try. I believed in my mind it was a safer environment for me, and I felt as though Faye and I were on the same level.

24

My girlfriend watched my son as I worked through the week. She worked at a garage on the weekends cleaning. This situation worked great for both of our schedules and helped me with daycare expenses.

One night, Nina called from work. "Whatcha doing?" she asked.

"Nothing, what's up?"

"Well, I'm on my break, and just wanted to call and see if you would mind if I brought a guy home after work. Would that be ok?"

"Sure, we can get the party started when you guys get here," I said.

"Yay! Sounds good. I'll see you soon."

A few hours later, Nina arrived with the guy she had been seeing. He was a lovely dresser and very polite. I invited him to sit down, and I made him a drink. I noticed his pockets being full when he came in the door. Before he could sit, this guy had rolls of money he had to take out to sit comfortably. I thought my eyes would pop out of my head; I had never seen that amount of money at one time in my life.

"Have you ever done cocaine?" he asked, as if it were no big deal.

"No, I don't think that is something I can afford." I chuckled. I could barely pay for my son's needs, much less an expensive drug.

"Well, tonight it is on me." He drew a line across my coffee table. I had no idea at the time what I was getting into, I only knew that I was all for something different and exciting.

Cocaine gave me a euphoric feeling. I had never felt anything like it. It gave me energy and put me in deep thought about everything. After the first time trying it, I was hooked. My thoughts raced to come up with a solution of how I would pay for my next line of cocaine. Within months I had lost over fifty pounds, and my hair was falling out. The days of barely eating were taking their toll on my body.

Rico, Nina's boyfriend, came over regularly. One day Rico stopped by and could tell something was wrong with me. I was irritable and quick with my answers.

"What can I do to help you?" he asked with concern, hiding a terrible plan. I was working a minimum wage job, and keeping up with my habit was getting tough. I expressed that to him.

"I know how you can make money and make it quick," he said. He sat me down to explain the details. "I will send you on an airline flight to a certain state. You will go through the airport dressed casually and comfortably. You will then go to the hotel I pick for you and wait for someone to knock. When you answer the door, there will be no extra conversation; no names shared, no extra anything. Take the package. The following day you will fly back through a different airline with the package on your person. No jewelry, no belts. I want you to be there dressed as a businesswoman. Dress like a pure, upstanding citizen; don't wear anything that will make the metal detector go off, understood?"

I had never flown before but understood the instructions I had been given. "Ok, Rico, let's do it. You let me know when you have everything ready for me to go, and I will make it happen."

It didn't take long for Rico to follow through with the plan.

My first flight was scary, but I followed instructions precisely, and to my surprise, it worked! A few weeks later I would return on another flight to a different location. A few times after doing this, I had all my bills paid and was able to buy the first cut-off of the Kilo. This same scenario would happen every trip, just to a different location.

Months later, I was scheduled to take a trip. It would be to a small airport terminal close to the Mexican border. I had done everything that I was told. The following day when I arrived at the airport, I noticed only one gate going in and one gate going out. With this terminal being smaller, it would be harder for me to blend into a crowd. I placed my bag on the conveyor belt to run through the X-ray machine. Only overnight things were in the bag, so this was routine for me. As I stepped through the metal detector, a loud siren went off, and my heart raced as if I had just been injected with epinephrine. "Stand over here, please," the border patrol agent stated.

I immediately began to pray in my head to the One that I had never called on: "Lord, If you get me out of this, I promise I will never do it again."

I was scared, and a vast lump was in my throat as I stepped to the side. The officer took the metal detector wand down in front of my person. They waved it up and down, but it made no sound. The border patrol told me that I could get my carry-on bag and proceed to my flight.

I could finally exhale. It was a huge relief.

When I got on the plane, I ran the checklist through my brain. I know that I didn't have any metal items on, so why in the world did I make the detector go off? I wondered. These thoughts ran through my mind as I headed back to my intended destination.

When I arrived, Rico was there to pick Nina and me up and take us to a safe location where the Kilos would be weighed, tested, and broken down. I explained to him what had happened at the airport and that I was not sure I could make another trip for him. I didn't want to. The detector going off had shaken me to my core.

Rico told me we'd figure it out, and not to freak out. We would find a way that I could work for him without having to go through an airport.

When we arrived at our destination, Rico cut open the Kilo and found on the backside a tiny square of aluminum foil. Someone was out to get him, but in turn, they would have also captured me in the process.

I explained to Rico that I felt that it just wasn't safe for me to take another flight. I avoided upsetting him by offering to sell in the clubs or to move marijuana instead of taking flights for cocaine. Because of the situation and how things went down, he was willing to let me go that route and make money that way.

CHAPTER SIX

A Call for Reprieve

My mom and I still kept a distant relationship. I would keep her at arm's length and allow her to come and take her grandson for the weekend. She explained that she would take him to church and teach him about Jesus. My mom had, in recent years, married yet again to a "Christian" man and was on what I called the "holy roller coaster." I thought this could be just a phase that Mama was going through at the time. Perhaps she was trying a Christian man this time in hopes of having a different result than all the times before. Who knew? I was tired of guessing what her intentions were. I just knew that for me, I was not going to have anything to do with it if I could help it. The less drama I had from her or her men, the better off I would be.

I recall that spring was approaching, and my mom had been inviting me to church for Easter. I had put her off for months, giving her every reason I could provide. Every weekend when she came to get my son, she would ask.

"Everyone seems to go to church on Easter," she would say.

I finally gave in to her requests. "Ok, Mama. I'll go on Easter Sunday."

Surely, this wasn't going to be weird for me. All the heathens go to church on Easter if they don't go any other time of the year.

A couple of weeks before Easter, I had hit bottom. Selling in the clubs and keeping up with my habit seem to take a turn for the worse. Trying to get that same euphoric feeling was not happening, and bills got behind again. My power had been cut off, and the rent was due. When I came down from being high, I had an extreme sense of hopelessness.

"No one cares if anything happened to me, so why even try?" I would think to myself.

I remember stepping into the kitchen crying. My son was in his room watching a cartoon. I hit my bedroom door angrily for letting myself get like this. Faye and Nina would be out of town, so I had nothing in front of me but an image of an ugly woman staring back at me who had made a mess of her life. How did I get myself into this situation?

Dropping to my knees on the kitchen floor, I grabbed a butcher knife out of the drawer. Laying it across the inside of my wrist, I could hear a voice inside my head saying, Do it! Nobody cares if anything happens to you anyway. You know you will be better off not feeling this pain anymore. I began to bear down with tears streaming down my face when suddenly a different voice pierced my pain: "Mommy, please don't do it!"

I looked up, and my son was standing there, still in a pull-up diaper and crying his little eyes out for his mommy who had lost all hope. His voice crying out to me shook my senses, and I dropped the knife to the floor. I put my arms around him.

"I'm sorry, baby. Mama is so sad right now. It's ok. Mama's not going to do it."

I called my mom but I didn't tell her about my crisis. Instead, I confessed that my power had been cut off because I was unable to pay the bill. She offered to come and get my son for a few days, which I accepted.

Now alone, I went through the motions, eating canned food and items that did not require power.

I took his plastic swimming pool and placed it in the backyard. I filled it with water in the morning for the sun to warm during the day, and come nightfall, I would bathe in it.

The next day a friend would call me and invite me to her party. Thankfully, it wasn't one of the bridges I had burned; she would have my back if I needed something to get high. At the party, they were smoking cocaine, and she offered me a little piece. I can remember hitting a soda can with tiny holes in it. When I struck the lighter to the can, I could hear what I thought was my conscience talking to me. "Remember, you made a promise to your mom. Tomorrow is Easter, and if you don't show, you will not hear the end of it."

I immediately panicked and told my friend I had to go home. I knew it would take a few hours to wind down after smoking.

I lay in my bed for hours and eventually fell asleep. The next day I woke up late and had an hour's drive to my mom's church. I had not worn a dress in years other than to a wedding, but I tried to clean myself up, putting on my best church face. I remember thinking that this service was probably going to be the longest two hours of my life.

I arrived at the church late, of course. I walked into the vestibule and could hear the choir singing. Those words that came from the sanctuary were piercing my heart to its core. I immediately began to cry as an usher approached me. "Ma'am, can I help you to your seat?"

"Yes please," I said. "My mother and stepfather are members here. Can you show me where they sit?" I followed him down the aisle to the front of the church. My stepfather was sitting there. My mom was in the choir.

Looking up there at my mom, I noticed she had a strange look on her face, almost as if she was wondering who this woman was sitting in the pew with her husband. Tears would not stop flowing. No one had to tell me about my life and what I was doing wrong. I knew. I realized there was a void in my life and I was at the end of my rope. The choir came down after a few moments, and as my mom got closer she realized it was me. Her mouth flew open as if she were in shock.

"You came! What's wrong? Are you ok?" I knew my mascara was running and I looked like an Alice Cooper wannabe. "Mama, I'm miserable," I said.

During the whole service, my mind raced with emotions. If I try to change, what will I do if I slip up? How can I even try to be good when I've been so used to being bad? Every excuse presented itself as the preacher was speaking. The altar call came and I held tightly onto the pew as if I was riding a motorcycle. I was not letting go. Every word that came out of the preacher's mouth was immediately answering the questions that I was asking myself.

"Some of you at this very moment are asking yourself how you can live this life," he said, "and you cannot do it all on your own. But Jesus inside you can help you in every situation. "He will give you hope when there is none."

All of a sudden, I let go of that pew and with no more reservations I ran down to the altar, pouring my words out to God.

"God I'm so sorry for what I've done! Please forgive me. I can't do this life anymore."

The preacher's wife talked me through my questions while at the altar and she gave me a Bible. After that, something was different inside of me, and the load I had been carrying suddenly felt so much lighter. I didn't know how I was going to live this new life I had taken on that day. What I did know is it had to be better than the one I had been living so far.

On the way home from church, I knew I wanted to break it off with my girlfriend. This was going to be a task. I just knew it wasn't who I was, and I no longer had the desire to be in that relationship. For me, something so strong inside was longing to be held by a different force and I knew that dating a woman was not the answer for me, nor were the drugs.

The answer was Jesus.

When we arrived back at the house, my son, who had been with me that morning and witnessed my conversion, immediately shouted to Faye with excitement, "Mama got saved today!"

I couldn't mirror his excitement because of the hard conversation that I knew was coming. Also, there was a faint smell of drugs in the house and I knew that Faye had been smoking marijuana.

Instantly, the look on her face dropped to the floor. "So what does this mean for us?" she asked.

My response was quick. "This means there can't be any more of this relationship. I know this isn't who I am."

Her anger was immediate, and her words were ugly. "So now you're gonna try to be a holy roller like your mom?" she asked, outraged. "Boy, you ain't gonna last long, I can tell you that!"

But I wasn't willing to let Faye's prediction come true.

I ran to the bedroom, called my mom, and told her I had to get out of there. If I didn't leave that environment, I was going to end up back into drugs and back into misery. I just couldn't stay. I was scared to death but had to see what this new life was about. Something in me was so free and this was a feeling I had never felt before. I had been in a mental prison for so long, and I certainly didn't want to stay there. If I did, I was going to end up dead.

A few days later my mom and stepdad were there with a truck to load our things. I was on my way to try to build a better life for myself and my son. With my parents' help, I could be on my feet in just a few months. At that moment, I had no idea what was to come. The only thing that I did know was that this man Jesus and His love for me changed my life and the feelings I carried inside. He was relentlessly pursuing every part of me, and in return, I had to find out who I was meant to be.

CHAPTER SEVEN
A New Start

After moving in with my mom and stepdad, I was able to get a job at a local hosiery mill. Working there was an adjustment from my previous life. Receiving legitimate pay was a relief in that I did not have to look over my shoulder continuously. Earning an honest living felt good to me. I could lay my head down at night and know I had done my best. I hoped that in just a few short months I would have enough money to move and find a place of my own in the area.

What I didn't realize was my world would soon be turned upside down.

My mom and step-dad went to church regularly. Since asking Jesus into my heart, I wanted to be there every chance I could. I read the Bible that was given to me on Easter daily. Some of the words I did not understand, and yet others were life-giving. I pulled them into my heart as much as possible.

Looking back on it now, some of what I was learning was very religious, meaning it was based on man-made rules rather than the Bible, yet some of it was a set of very crucial spiritual tools that I would need in the months to come. I was thankful for it all. Without those tools, I wouldn't have been able to make it emotionally when they arrested me.

I got saved before my arrest. I had no idea that they were investigating the people that I worked with illegally. All I knew when I got clean was that I needed to get out of the environment I was in or I would be tempted to go back to those old people, places, and things. That bad, previous life was something I knew. It was familiar. And it would be all too easy to go back.

I thought that life after accepting Christ and receiving His love would somehow get easier. That was not the case. While I did have joy and peace inside that I had never felt before, life itself got harder. The US Marshals would soon come and arrest me, but through all of this Jesus and His love for me would never stop.

I'm not exactly sure why we think that life gets easier when we make a profession of faith. My thinking at that moment was that life was easy for Christians because I saw smiles on their faces and happiness for a lot of the ones that said they knew Jesus. I automatically assumed that life was easy for them and that prosperity would follow for me as well.

CHAPTER EIGHT

The Day of Reckoning

When the US Marshals arrested me, I knew immediately my past had come to haunt me. They picked me up from my parents' house and escorted me to an SUV. An agent from the State Bureau of Investigation (SBI) warned, "Watch your head," as she assisted me in getting into the dark undercover vehicle.

A car pulled into the driveway as the arrest was taking place. My step dad and my son stepped out of the car. Seeing my son's tear-filled eyes framed by his adorable chubby cheeks pierced my heart like nothing ever before. "Mama! Don't take my mama!" he cried. He was begging for his mama to stay, but I knew it wasn't going to happen.

On the way to jail, the SBI agent questioned me. "What do you know concerning this person?" She flashed a photo book at me with a mug shot of a person I had never seen. My reply came quickly, "I don't know them."

She then proceeded to ask familiar things. My response was clear and respectful. "Ma'am, I know you get this all the time, but I'm drug-free now. I have changed my life. Ask my son what kind of mama I am now—he knows the difference. If you ask me any questions about others, I will have to look over my shoulder for the rest of my life. If you ask about myself, I'll be honest about what I did."

The rest of the drive was in silence.

The closer we got to the jail, I began to recognize my surroundings. This city was a little over an hour from where they had arrested me. My handcuffs were rubbing my wrists, but I dared not to complain. I was scared to death.

"Stand here please," a lady deputy said as I approached a wall with height measurements on it. "Turn to the side please. . . and to the other."

I couldn't believe this was happening. I felt as if my life was flashing before my eyes as the deputy asked a list of questions. "Do you have any scars?" Yes ma'am. "Do you have any tattoos?" Yes ma'am. I made sure my responses were direct, precise, and respectful. These people *had* to know that I didn't belong here. I was different. The woman that once was, had been buried, never to return.

"Ma'am," I said, "May I ask a question? Do you have a Bible that I can read?"

The woman stepped into a side room for a brief moment and came back. She handed me a paperback bible. It had neither front nor back cover. It had illuminated pages in between. Several inmates before had used this book. I was grateful to have it. It was going to be my lifeline in the days, months, and years to come.

After I was booked, another deputy came to take me to my cell. She warned me that this was one of the toughest jails in North Carolina and to keep one eye open at all times. Fear of what could happen swelled inside me.

When we came to the pod, I could see different floors with stairs. A pod was an enclosed living area that would house a certain number of inmates. Girls looked through a slit of a window as the deputy escorted me into the living area. In my arms were generic hygiene items, a small plastic comb, a motel-style soap, a tiny toothbrush, deodorant, and toothpaste. I was given a fitted sheet and a wool blanket. The green wool blanket was scratchy in my arms.

The deputy stated that these cells could house two to four inmates at a time depending on how full the jail population was. I shuffled along in prison-issued orange flip-flops and a navy blue jumpsuit, my heart pounding. We approached my cell, and I noticed that next to the door was a clipboard with a short wooden pencil attached to a piece of yarn. I looked closer and there was a sheet of paper on the clipboard with the name JESUS written in pencil on it. When I asked what this clipboard was used for, the deputy stated it was for when someone was not feeling well. Inmates were to sign their names on it and would be called sometime that day to be checked out medically. But the name Jesus? Sure, there were men named Jesús in Spanish-speaking communities—but these inmates were all women! Why in the world would the name Jesus be on there? I suddenly felt a peace that the Lord was speaking to my heart and that the message on that clipboard was meant for me.

"Corinna."

Yes, Lord?

"I am here with you; I haven't left."

I was the first inmate to enter the cell. Thankfully no one was in there for me to worry about arguments or worse—fighting physically. I was on a twenty-three-hour lockdown. I had one hour in the morning to get breakfast, stretch, and shower.

Over the next seven days, I would have nothing to do but think. So many thoughts and questions ran through my mind. I worried about how I would transfer custody of my son to my mom. I knew I was going to prison for a while, but I was more specifically concerned as to how much time I would get behind bars. My sentencing guidelines showed I could pull up to ten years.

After several days of being in jail, one of the correction officers—called COs—tapped on my cell door.

"Holland."

"Yes, Ma'am," I replied.

"They are bringing you a roommate and she is an accessory to murder." Thoughts and emotions ran through me quickly. It was as if I had just been placed in front of a firing squad. Fear pierced my soul. I was overwhelmed by the information from the CO. Questions rang in my head with a survival checklist. Am I gonna have to fight this girl? I wondered. The next few moments could be crucial, and I knew that.

Minutes later the cell door unlocked and this giant of a woman entered the room. Throwing her mat to the floor she turned toward me and stood staring at the Bible in my lap. "Are you a Christian?" she asked.

With a lump in my throat, I answered, "Yes, I am."

Immediately a rejoicing sound came from her! "Thank you Lord for sending me a Christian roommate!" she exclaimed. "God had to put me flat on my back to get my attention!" She explained further, "I got saved at a service here at the jail two years ago. My boyfriend killed someone, and I was in the wrong place at the wrong time. I am still here waiting to be sentenced and taken to prison."

Once the air was cleared and introductions were made, we talked about Jesus and how he had spared both our lives, and that night we had church. No steeple, no altar: just a cell and two redeemed women with a tattered bible. She shared her heart with me that day and it was so encouraging for me. I have often asked myself if she was an angel that visited me. I cannot remember her name or recall her face. The one thing that I do recall is the peace that I felt when she entered the room. The feeling was so serene. I could have stayed in that cell so much longer with her being there with me. Jesus was showing me more of His love without conditions every day, and if He could use a donkey or a burning bush, He could use this lady.

The next morning the feds were going to pick me up for my first court appearance. I was to be given a court-appointed attorney to see if the judge would allow me out on a pre-trial basis. Before I left, my roommate asked, "Can I give you a scripture, Baby Girl? I need you to learn Romans 8:28." This particular verse reads as follows: "And we know all things work together for good to those who love God, who are called according to His purpose." She said, "You plant this word in your heart, and you stand on it while you are doing your time. It's gonna carry you through."

The federal agents picked me up from the local county jail where I had been held over. They placed a chain around my waist which was linked to a chain with cuffs around my ankles. The cuffs around my wrists were then tied to the chain around my waist. It was difficult taking tiny little steps trying to get into the courthouse. Several other inmates were placed in this chain gang with me, a long train of inmates all tied together with chains and stocks. All the other inmates were quiet during this time as you had to concentrate to be able to walk and not trip.

I was then placed in a holding cell. It was like a see-through cage. Once they placed me inside, I was able to sit and wait.

Time stood still. What lay ahead for me was to be determined by the judge. Since I had been arrested, twenty-eight other co-defendants had been denied the chance to be out on a bond. These were other people waiting to be charged in the same court case. Knowing their bond had been denied, my lawyer and I were taking a step of faith. He had explained that we could at least try for pretrial, which is a period of being allowed out while waiting for my court hearing. It would allow me to handle my personal affairs before my sentencing. It didn't look great for me since all of the others had been denied. Only God knew what was to come.

A female US Marshal came around the corner towards where I was. "Ms. Holland, the judge is going to let you go home today on a non-secure bond. They have gone to get you some clothes that you can change into."

What? Is she serious? I thought. I wanted to cry.

They got me out of the holding cell and took me into where the judge's chambers were. The judge agreed for me to have a court-appointed attorney and then made me aware that I was going to be able to leave with just a signature. No money had to be put down for my release on pre-trial. That day only a signature from my step-father was required. Of course, this also made him the responsible party if I failed a drug test or no-showed to any court dates. I felt the burden of needing to handle my personal affairs before my sentencing, and doing everything right so that my step dad didn't have any consequences.

In the next few months, I continued to work and save money. I knew that I would need to leave this money with my mom and step dad to help as much as possible with my son while I was away. I had Mom placed as Power of Attorney (POA) with authority over decisions about my son. My oldest brother, Duane, would be the backup in case something happened to my mom and she wasn't able to take care of him. Little did I realize at the time that everything that I so carefully planned would be wiped away.

My pretrial officer would come and visit once a month while out on release. She would place a sweat patch on me and come to retrieve it in about four weeks. This sweat patch would drug test my body over a continual thirty-day period. Repeatedly every month was the same scenario until the day drew near for sentencing.

Stepping into the courtroom with my attorney, I noticed that there were two of my co defendants to be charged at the same time as myself. I had never heard of anything like this before. The judge proceeded to ask questions to the others.

"Do you have anything that you would like to say to the court?" he asked. Both of their heads hung down, shook left and right, and they had no words. They were both sentenced to two separate 60-month sentences, the first sixty months for perjury, and the other sixty months for drug conspiracy. My knees were knocking together as if it were fifteen below zero inside the courtroom.

The judge looked at me and directed the same question to me. But my answer was different.

"Your Honor, yes. I would like to apologize to the court for my actions. I would also like to apologize to my family for what I have done and what I am about to put them through. Your Honor, I promise no matter how much time you give me, I will share my story with others so they don't make the same mistakes I have made."

The judge looked down at my paperwork and then back at me. "Alright, Ms. Holland. I'm gonna allow you to take the drug program while in prison. That will take a year off your sentence with an allowed 6 months at a halfway house. I'm going to sentence you with 32 months."

Immediately I knew the Lord had His continued covering over my life. I was somehow thankful and sad all at the same time because I knew that day I was not going home. It was time to face my demons.

CHAPTER NINE

God Wink

I learned a little bit about imprisonment over the seven days I had spent in the county jail after being arrested and before I went out on pretrial. Now I had been sentenced and was being held in jails in the area. I might have been at one facility for a few weeks and then would be transferred to another. This was not for the faint of heart and I knew that. I could never understand how there could be "career criminals." This was mental torture, but I knew that I needed to pull my chin up and take care of this for the things I had done. I had heard the cliché, "You do the crime, you do the time," more times than I cared to count, but it was the truth—the brutal truth.

One of the jails I was held over at was small. It had no windows or daylight that came in. This reminded me of a dungeon. Seven cells were on the women's side. They were electric and would open when they wanted someone or to let us come out for one hour to eat and shower. So I spent long hours in my cell, and I had to keep my mind busy. At times I could hear others through the wall on the men's side. One day they could be fighting and stirring up a stink, and the next day I could hear singing or rapping. I never could tell how the day was going to go as far as that was concerned; it fluctuated a lot.

Soon enough, Christmas was around the corner and the inmates were a ball of emotions. I could hear Christmas carols through the wall and silence came over the jail. The harmonic sounds and acoustics through the jail were amazing. That fleeting moment of remembering Jesus' birth and all that entailed flooded my heart with bittersweet joy and tenderness. Late into the night for what seemed like hours, different songs came through the wall, and the girls on my side would join in.

One of the female deputies at the jail was named Millie. She was short and stout. She dyed her hair super dark brown and penciled in her eyebrows to match. Once upon a time her hair could have been that shade, as it suited her features. She had this sweet, kind Southern Belle accent, but could get stern when she knew someone was trying to take advantage of her.

Several days a week we had pinto beans. Pinto bean casserole, or refried beans and corn. Your mouth did not want to eat it, but you needed to, or you would be famished by supper time. Millie would offer an extra cup of kool aid to wash the beans down with. From the many small acts of kindness Millie presented to me as well as the other girls, we knew something was different about her. This was especially true at Christmas time.

During this Christmas season, Millie came into our block late one night as I heard the electric door open and then close back.

"Ladies, I want to tell you that it is snowing outside, and if you behave, I will take you one by one to see it." I could hear girls in their cells jumping up out of the beds with excitement.

Sad sighs and sobs one by one as they returned. Something so simple, yet so profound, was the love that this deputy was showing all of us.

"Are you ready Ms. Holland?"

"Yes ma'am," I replied.

She took me through a door down a long hallway. We waited for another door to be opened. Once we were able to go through, I could see a tiny window to the right as we got closer.

"Ok, you can look. I will give you just a minute." She stepped to the side as I had to slightly stand on my tiptoes to see out of the window.

And there it was, in all its majesty. Snow falling and white as far as my eyes could see. Nothing disturbed my view. I must have been looking out a window at the backside of the jail. Tree limbs drooped with several inches of beautiful white, lush stacks of snow. The ground was covered and glistened with iridescent tones.

I found myself weeping quietly, staring at the beauty that God had placed before me. My eyes had not seen daylight nor the outdoors for a few months. In the stillness of the fallen snow, I felt the Lord's touch in a way that I cannot explain. The peace I felt at that moment and the gift that the deputy had given me could not have been bought with any money, for she had shown me the face of God. She loved me when I felt that no one else did. What beauty to behold in His creation—both the beauty of Millie's kindness, and the fresh blanket of snow on the ground.

Shortly after we left that window and went back to my cell.

I began to sing a sweet melody about Jesus giving his life and promising hope to everyone who believes.

The space filled with the echo and my tears poured down as I sang the sweetest song unto Him. He had me and everything around me. That was my reminder, yet again, that I was not alone.

CHAPTER TEN

Caught in the Crossfire

A few weeks later I was picked up by the Feds. They were finally taking me to prison, and I just knew it had to be better than the temporary jail where I was being held. At least I would get to move around. This was a working prison camp that they were taking me to. Even for only fifteen cents an hour, at least it was something to keep me busy.

Several more weeks passed, and I finally received approval to call home. I had been longing to hear my son's voice or his laughter. My inmate account funds finally arrived from the jail I was at previously, so I could pay for the call. I had already placed a lot on my mom and stepdad, so as long as I could, I would pay for my calls to speak to him. After several attempts to call, I still wasn't getting an answer or the phone call would be denied. What in the world is going on? I thought to myself. I had so many unanswered questions, and the more I called, the more discouraged I became.

About the same time, I received a job at the local hospital on the compound. It was a bandaid station for different complaints that the inmates had. For example, if an inmate came in complaining of a migraine, they would administer tylenol and tell them to return if it continued.

I learned to do industrial waxing, buffing, and mopping floors. I took pride in the work I did, and my floors looked as if you could eat your next meal off of them.

One day I was buffing the floor when an officer came to me and told me that I had a legal phone call that I needed to take. I was escorted down the hill to the main campus where I was taken to a counselor's office.

I picked up the phone and a woman began to speak. "Ms. Holland, I needed to make you aware that your son has been placed in foster care. He was turned over to us just a few days ago."

My heart fell.

"What happened? Why is he there?" I asked frantically, the beating of my heart pounding hard in my chest.

The woman explained that my mom had given my son up to my oldest brother, as he was my backup power of attorney in case something happened to my mom. She told me that my brother's neighbor had watched him for a few hours. The neighbor's son and my son were playmates and went to the same school. When they were playing outside in warmer weather, she had offered him a short sleeve shirt that he could play in. When she pulled up a sleeve she found him covered in bruises all over his arms and legs and immediately called social services, as it was apparent that he had been abused.

My reaction was pure Mama Bear outrage. "Duane needs to take this out on me instead of my son! It is not his fault! You wait until I get out of here! He's gonna have to face me!"

Feelings of anger, confusion, and frustration were all tied into one. I could not understand why this was happening. I thought Duane and Mama loved him. I thought they loved me. It did not help my frustration with the situation that I had no contact with anyone and felt clueless about what had happened. I was let down and enraged by both of them.

I went into action immediately. I wrote letters to everyone I could. I wrote letters to caseworkers, pleading on my son's behalf for them to please not take custody away from me. I agreed that my family had done this to him, but that I had no idea that they were capable of that type of abuse towards him when I gave him into their custody.

A few months later, I received a certified letter stating that the foster family that he had been placed with was wanting to adopt him.

What in the world was I going to do?

A woman from the church I attended wrote me a letter stating that she was taking foster care classes and that she would be attending the next court date to see if she could get custody of my son. She had been through many things in recent years with cancer and was a retired RN, but he knew Barbara from church.

She had the kindest heart and would love him to the best of her ability. It was hard to fathom, but it would be a good thing.

As the days passed all I could think of was what my child was going through or thinking. Does he think his Mama is not coming back for him? No way was I going to sit idly by and do this time without trying to write every person I could.

On the date of court, it was all I could think about. I got through cleaning the hospital and only a couple of hours had passed. I couldn't call the woman from church until after what they called 'count', which was when they counted the prisoners. I also needed to make sure to go to chow, or I would be starving by the time 'bed count' came. The prison camp had two main counts a day that we needed to be concerned with: Four o'clock in the afternoon after all areas of the compound got off work, and the stand-up bedtime count at nine o'clock at night. I would go get chow and then come back to my unit to get in line to call.

"Barbara, how are you? Man, my day has been dragging and it seemed like forever before I could call."

Speaking in a nervous chatter, Barbara interrupted me. "Corinna, are you going to let me tell you about how the day went?"

"Yes, of course!"

She explained the things that had happened to my son in recent months. She told me she pleaded with the judge, telling him that I had no idea that my family could have allowed this to happen. She then explained that she had taken foster certification and that she would like to have custody of my son Cody while I was incarcerated and that she would love him. That day the judge let her have custody, and she would soon bring him to see me at the prison. I was yelling with joy from the top of my lungs at the phone booth! Take that devil! You didn't win!

The prison was putting on a Family Day soon where mothers could spend the day with their children. That was a day that I was so looking forward to. Weeks down the road, Family Day finally came and I got up early to be sure that I would look my very best for him. We were going to be able to take pictures and have food with our children. They finally called me to the visiting center.

I would have to go through the security room going in and then again going back, but I didn't care what kind of strip search or security check I was going to have to go through. All I knew was I wanted my arms around my little one, to let him know that mama had not given up on him, nor would she ever give up on getting him back.

I came through the door and looked across the room. There was my sweet, chunky monkey running towards me. I scooped him up into my arms and did not want to let him go. His smell, his laugh, his hug. All of those things that I used to take for granted. I was sure that I would never do that again. This was the first day that I had held him since I had been sentenced nearly a year before. The visit ended too soon that day, but it gave me such a drive to finish my race well and do my time and not let it do me.

A few months later I received word from Barbara that having my son had placed a toll on her body physically and mentally. She realized that taking this on was more than what her health would allow. I thanked her for the time that she could foster and understood that she just could not do anymore. She had already done more than most, and I was grateful for that.

Soon, he was placed into a loving foster family that allowed me to crochet things for him and write as often as I wanted. This was a lifeline for me and gave me hope that one day I would have him again.

My sentence did eventually come to an end, and I was scheduled to be taken to a halfway house. I was given fifteen dollars and a bus ticket home. I had on a jogging suit and the shoes on my feet. I didn't care at the time that I didn't have anything else; I would worry about that when I got to where I was going.

When I arrived at the halfway house, I was still considered to be in the custody of the Bureau of Prisons. I was required to obtain work within seven days with the consequence that I would return to prison to finish the remainder of my sentence if I remained unemployed.

I got a job at a local company doing housekeeping on third shift. It wasn't much, but at least it was something and was an honest living. I could not complain. I was grateful to be out in the world and not doing time in a facility somewhere.

I worked hard and saved money and bought a cheap car. Soon I found a little two bedroom trailer to rent. I bought pieces of furniture here and there from the local Goodwill so I could have my home ready for when I was released. All I could think of was trying to get Cody back.

On the day of my release from the halfway house I had a court date a few counties away where Cody lived with his foster family. The counselor spoke up for me and told the judge that she wished she had more mothers that worked as hard and diligently as I did. The judge said he could see that I had learned my lesson and that he would give my son back to me.

CHAPTER ELEVEN
The Healing Begins

My son and I settled in quite nicely. I continued to work as a housekeeper. It was hard to even think about trying to get another job. Being a felon, I would need to hold on to this job as long as I could.

I had not heard from my mom in over two years. I missed her but never understood why all that stuff happened while I was in prison. I was hurt and angry. I would protect my son until my life on earth was finished, that I was sure of. The many years of pain that she had caused and the situations that I always seemed to be in with her left me confused and hurt, yet at the same time, my heart longed for a relationship with her.

As the end of October approached, my church announced that there would be an event on Halloween at the coliseum and that the kids would receive a bag of candy. Some southern gospel groups would be singing at this event.

I took my son and greeted one of the members of my church when I noticed him there. I was kind of surprised when he said he was looking for me. "Corinna, you are not going to believe this. I just saw your mom! Why don't you go and speak to her?"

My heart sank.

"Look, there are twenty thousand people here, and she is not going to cause a scene in front of everyone."

"If she is mean, just tell her you love her, and walk away. It's that simple," he said.

The way he explained that to me, knowing I had a way to escape if I felt things were going badly, I knew that going to find her was safe because I was in a public environment. I proceeded to follow him to the area where he had seen her. She was coming through the corridor as we were approaching. She brushed shoulders with me and passed by without recognizing me. The guy looked at me as I shrugged my shoulders.

"We are not going to let her go without talking to you!" he exclaimed.

He walked up from behind, tapped her on the shoulder and asked, "Judy, aren't you going to speak to your daughter?"

Her mouth fell open and she began to cry, "My baby, my baby." But I had walls up and had to keep a distance. I, nor Cody, would ever be hurt again by her or Duane if I could help it. At the time, all I could offer her was my phone number. I felt like that was all I could give and at least it was something. Too many questions were left unanswered. So much pain on and off for so many years. Was it that she loved me the best way she knew how, even though that type of love seemed so toxic? I didn't know; the only thing I knew was the little girl inside longed to be loved by her mama.

Before I knew it, Christmas time was approaching and our church would be performing a play named "I Dreamed I Searched Heaven For You". Cody and I both had parts in the play, and I felt that this could be a good neutral ground to invite Mama to come and see us perform.

Opening night, the pews were filled. I could see Mama sitting in one of the front pews. My character in the play went to Heaven, which would be located in the choir loft at the front of the church. I could see tears pouring down Mama's face throughout the night. My actual thought was, Man, this play is good, but it is not *that* good, as I watched her pull tissues from her purse.

At the end of the play, my pastor gave an altar call. The altar was filled with people crying their hearts out to God for change in their life. I watched my mom proceed out from the pew and walk to the bottom of the stairs at the foot of the altar. She reached out her hands to gesture for me to come to her. When I got there the words poured from her lips with such sincerity that my heart melted.

"I'm so sorry for what I've put you through. My marriage turned into a shambles after you left for prison. I thought I was doing the right thing by giving custody of Cody to Duane. I had no idea he would hurt him in any way. I am so sorry for all the things in your life that were a mess. I never meant to hurt you."

Tears ran down my face. I embraced my Mama for what felt like the first time. I needed to hear those words. I didn't want to hold on to the pain anymore. The load was so heavy that I could not carry it.

This was the beginning of a beautiful mother-and-daughter relationship. Learning how to love and be loved was life-changing. Was it easy? No. But we were intentional with our relationship and wanted more than ever to be in each other's lives. I think my mom realized that day who she was after spending all those years trying to fill a void of being loved. I think she finally realized that through Christ she was already enough and she could not be loved by Him more than she was at that very moment.

Laying the hurt down was a release for us both. I think it also helped me to see her through a different lens. Looking into my reflection at the forgiveness that was applied to me, while never doing anything to deserve it, helped me to see her. My heart hurt for her. I longed for her to know that the identity she was seeking through relationships kept her hiding behind a man. When she came to know Jesus' love and the freedom that it brought, she was no longer concerned with her flesh and dysfunctional relationships.

I gave Mama my address and after that we would see each other regularly. She would come for coffee or dinner or we'd go shopping. One day I received a call from Mama stating that Duane had been placed in the ICU. He had chronic pancreatitis. All the years of drinking had taken their toll and they were not expecting him to pull through. Mama stated that she would leave the decision up to me as to whether I would go and visit him or not. I'm not going to sugarcoat this: it was hard. A part of me wanted to have revenge for what he did to Cody, and a part of me wanted to weep for my brother. I thought of what internal pain must have led him to this life, and I thought about why things ever had to happen this way.

I decided to go see him. With the diagnosis of pancreatitis as well as being HIV positive, I was afraid I would not see him again and did not want to live with that on my conscience.

When I got to the hospital room, I was at a loss for words. They had a tube as big as my pinky finger running through his nose into his stomach pumping out green bile. I stepped towards the bed and placed my hand on his. He opened his eyes and proceeded to speak.

"You've always been pretty, but now you are beautiful."

No words were spoken about what had happened. I did not have it in me. Forgiveness came without a word. I immediately saw him through a lens of love and all the junk didn't seem to matter anymore. What mattered to me was the here and the now. His words were so profound to me. I knew in my heart that the beauty he had seen and recognized was Jesus.

Duane had seen me before salvation and he could tell the difference. My relationship with Jesus was real and tangible, and

I could feel every day that same grace and mercy that He gave to me at the altar and that I am now giving to my loved ones. Looking in the mirror at my reflection after so many things I had done, how could I not love Duane the way Jesus loved me?

Duane came out of ICU several days later. They called him the Million Dollar Man for being in and out of the hospital so much. In later years he would be in and out several more times. He would have a leg amputated for osteomyelitis setting into the bone of one leg. But he was resilient and never gave up.

We never spoke about what he did to Cody. We never had to, honestly. I chose to forgive him whether he asked for it or not. Cody chose to forgive him as well. We focused only on family and the relationship between him and Mama. Life was so short, and we knew that.

Duane had a partial amputation of that same leg yet again. His sugar was out of control which would make it very difficult for that leg to heal. Duane had moved in with Mama and she would help take care of him as well as work her full-time job.

CHAPTER TWELVE

The Confirmation

I got married when Cody was eleven. The man I married had a testimony similar to mine. This was an exciting new journey for me. The fact that someone could love me enough to marry and give me their name was such a humbling feeling.

A year later I was pregnant and gave birth to a baby girl. There were thirteen years between their ages. Cody was an amazing big brother and helped me with her a lot.

Mama and I continued to have a relationship. She loved getting our daughter, Jayden, and having her spend the night. She mentioned that she was wanting to take her school shopping, so we planned a night for her to stay over. When I got there that Saturday morning, Mama had explained that she was having difficulty getting Duane to wake up. We had questioned whether he had taken too much pain medication due to his leg not yet being healed.

"Mama, let's go and see if we can get him up," I said. He needed to take some IV medications that day and had a PICC line for that. They were giving those to him as an outpatient.

Mama got a cold rag and wiped Duane's face as he had drool running down his chin. He was gurgling with every breath he was taking. He didn't say a word while she was wiping, but we could tell he was getting angry every time she wiped. He would make grunting sounds.

"Let me try Mama," I said, hoping to wake him so that he could get up and the morphine would wear off. When I wiped his face he opened his eyes and looked up at the ceiling and closed them back. "There you are!" I said. I told Mama he was fine and that he should be waking up soon with his eyes opening at that moment.

I finished my cup of coffee and left Jayden with Mama. I planned to pick her up the next day. Several minutes after I left, Mama called my cell phone. "Corinna, your brother isn't breathing! Turn around and come back! I'm calling 911!"

I immediately got off the next exit and looped around to head back to Mama. The whole trip back I was spent praying aloud for God to bring him back. When I got there Mama was in a straddle position on top of Duane doing CPR in order to use as much of her body weight as she could for compressions. At the same moment Mama was on speakerphone with 911. I could see Mama was out of breath as she was working on Duane. I told her to get down and that I would take over CPR until EMS got there. When EMS finally arrived they asked us to step out.

They did everything they could do for him, but it was too late. He was already gone.

Mama Skyped my brother Dickie to tell him the news. He lived in Wales, and we knew there would be no way he would be able to afford to fly home. Mama let Dickie see Duane and tell him bye. He needed closure and Mama knew that.

I went home that night, packed a bag and would head back to Mama in the morning. I would then help her go through his things and decide what we were going to do for his funeral.

That night I had a dream. I could see Duane's spirit leaving his body at the moment that he opened his eyes when I wiped his face. I had no idea that Duane had coded at that moment, but in my dream, I felt like the Lord was showing me that He had come to get him.

My emotions were all across the board. He was only six years older than me. Why did it have to be this way? I wondered to myself.

I knew in the days and years ahead I would need to look out for Mama. I knew how I felt as a sister, and I could not imagine what it would feel like as a mother laying her child to rest.

Mama and I were discussing the events that happened right before his passing. Duane had a friend visit him a couple of days before his death. Mama could hear her sharing her heart to Duane in his room. She shared that her husband had been very abusive to her. He had been drinking heavily the last several days, yelling and screaming at her in the process, and making her feel so useless. Mama overheard Duane ask her if he could pray for her and her situation. She heard, "Lord, we ask that you move on his heart, that he would be delivered from this alcohol."

Mama felt that in this prayer she knew that Duane had a personal relationship with God before his passing. There had been doubt because of many things he had said and done, but when he was asked if he had a personal relationship with God, he would confirm that with a yes. Between that and the prayer she overheard, it was enough to give us peace.

A few weeks later Mama went to the dentist and they found an abnormal place on her tongue. After running scans they diagnosed her with head and neck cancer. She would have surgery and then six weeks of chemo and radiation. I don't believe Mama could have taken care of Duane physically while battling cancer. During this time and many weeks after, Mama became weak and could barely eat due to the radiation burns in her mouth.

I lived forty-five minutes away from Mama. Weeks into treatment her weakness became more intense. I would pick her up on the days she had chemo. One day when picking her up, I could tell that she had been crying. She began to tell me about someone that she had met in the waiting area, she told them about Jesus and His love for them. I was amazed watching her go through the hardest battle and yet she still found strength, hope, and joy for her journey.

CHAPTER THIRTEEN
Crossroads

I was thirty when I got married. My husband JD was a felon who had a past of drug use and had been to prison twice. He had been recently released for the second time when I met him. His fire and zeal for the Lord were contagious. I was happy with being with a man that I felt I could relate to. After dating just a few months, we began telling our testimonies to local churches. Being with him gave me the feeling that my life had so much more meaning.

After the wedding, I learned quickly that being married to someone had its learning curves. Whether it was dealing with attitudes or bad habits, it took some getting used to, but I was all in when it came to being with a man that I loved and dedicated my life to. Two years into our marriage our daughter was born. Cody was great with her, and that allowed me to do daily tasks, even watching her so that I could take a shower. Having her at the age of thirty-two was a life change compared to having Cody at the age of nineteen.

A few years after our daughter was born, JD began to act differently. There would be moments where his story would not add up or I would even catch him in little white lies. One night he didn't come home. I was so angry and determined that I was going to find him. During the many late-night hours that I was driving up and down one of our main roads in the local town, I recalled JD telling me about a friend from his past and where he lived. I had met him once when the guy visited our church.

This old friend's driveway was covered with trees so it was not visible from the road. I pulled up into this driveway, got out, and went to knock on the door. I could hear voices from inside the house, but no one would answer. I headed back to the car where Jayden was in her car seat. Just then, JD's friend came out of the house. He was stuttering as he spoke, fumbling for words.

"Now Corinna, he ain't here now, don't start any trouble here and you just go back home." The more he spoke the angrier I got. I knew that JD must have been inside. I had a drink cup in my hand and threw it at him. My voice got louder as I spoke. "I am telling you right now that you better send him out! He needs to be home with his family!"

JD came out of the house hanging his head. "Now Corinna, calm down," he said. "This isn't what it looks like."

"Isn't what it looks like?" I responded. "How do you think it is supposed to look? You were supposed to be home four hours ago! You need to come home. I have been worried and the baby has been crying for you."

"You head home honey. I'm coming home, I promise."

I calmed down considerably. I got back into the car and headed home. I didn't need to have Jayden out in that mess anyway. I put Jayden down with me in the bed. If she cried or fussed I would be able to hear her. I was so exhausted mentally and physically. My mind continually played the hamster wheel. Hours passed and the morning came and still no sign of JD. He didn't want to be with us, and he clearly showed that by his actions.

It was several days before he came home. I had barely slept or eaten; I loved him so much and did not want to be alone. He offered apologies over and over and he explained that he had "slipped up"—those were his words for it.

A few days later we placed him into a local Christian rehab where he would go for three months to get himself together. The three months while he was gone I would hold our daughter when she cried for him.

"Mama, when is daddy coming home?"

"Soon baby, very soon."

Cody was the man of the house while his dad was gone. He helped me to watch Jayden while I cooked supper and cleaned. It wasn't easy, but I knew with the Lord's help that we would pull through.

JD came out of rehab with new hope and ready to tackle the world yet again. The kids were so happy. They had missed him so much, as had I. And he was good for a few years until the lies would begin again. He had such a hard time realizing that he could not dabble with friends from his past, for they did not have his best interest in mind and wanted nothing more than to see him fail.

We placed him into the same faith-based rehab. We visited him after a month on Sunday afternoons and in between visits we wrote to him. I longed for him to be set free from addiction and to be the person I knew that he could be. Once again, he came out of rehab and seemed to have his life back in order.

After everything that had happened, though, my marriage was shot. All I could think of when he left the home was where he was or what he was doing. My trust in him was gone. I loved him so much, but was that enough? I found out that it wasn't. It was going to take so much more than that. I could see that more every day.

I wanted this marriage to work. I just couldn't let him go with the thought that just maybe there was a hope that he might change for good.

Then the lies started again. He would not come home for days at a time just as he had done before he went to rehab the last time. I was so scared that I was going to receive a call that he was either dead from an overdose or the people that he had been dealing with had killed him. He and I separated. It was more than the lies and destructive behavior. I was scared that if anyone found out that he was using, I would lose our kids. If they thought that I was in on the addiction, or they heard about me losing Cody years before, it could be detrimental for me. I had already experienced that loss for what was really a brief moment in time, and I knew I could not do it again. JD had to get clean and stay that way.

I found a small trailer to rent in the area. I would get a few things from our house little bits at a time until I had enough to accommodate taking care of myself and Jayden. Cody moved out when he was eighteen and got married, so Jayden was my main concern at the moment.

One day when I thought JD was at work, I stopped by our house to pick up some dishes. With JD gone, I thought I could get a few things without any drama and then be on my way. I stepped into the kitchen to get a pan out of the bottom drawer of the stove and saw a shadow in my peripheral vision. When I turned, I looked down the hallway from the kitchen and noticed a head of hair coming out of the top of the covers.

"Who's here?" I said. No response. I stepped closer toward the bedroom to investigate. As I got closer I knew this was a female.

On the nightstand, I noticed a large light and what looked like a fairy wand, a spoon, and a needle. This female did not know that I was there. She had passed out from the drugs. My heart sank. JD had been cheating on me and there was no way I was coming back to him. Not with this.

Immediately, I filed separation papers at the courthouse. A year could not go by fast enough for me; I wanted out. I could not put my daughter through this anymore.

My covenant before God was real and I meant it. But what kind of line do you draw in the sand as to whether it's enough? Lord, what do I do? I didn't break my vow. He broke *his*. Was I perfect? No. But the one thing that I held so dear to me was disregarded, and I knew I couldn't do this anymore.

Experiencing three relapses in ten years, and then added to that his unfaithfulness, had ripped my heart into a million pieces.

I would have to wait a year until the date of separation. Nights were hard. Jayden and I would watch TV and just lie there. Once a week I would meet her dad at the local McDonalds for them to see each other for one hour. Sometimes he would show up but be several minutes late. Other times I would stay and wait for several minutes and he would never show. When they were visiting, I kept a distance in the restaurant but had my eye on every move that he made. I didn't trust him as far as I could throw him. My mission was to protect her and I would fight tooth and nail for her regardless of the circumstances.

Divorce is never easy for anyone involved. I tried my best to allow Jayden to have a relationship with her dad, but only if she wanted it. While he was actively using, I would only allow her to see him in a public area. It was important for me to allow her to see that even though I was angry at the things that he had put us through, I still wanted to try to get along and someday be able to forgive him.

As a newly single parent, I had to think everything through and budget every bit of money I made. I would allow this much for groceries one week and this much for lights. One day at a time was all I could see. But the more days that passed, the more I could feel that I was going to make it, by God's grace.

CHAPTER FOURTEEN

Tell Your Heart To Beat Again

After the divorce, I had sworn to myself that I would not get married again. It was too easy to get in and hard as ever to get out. Even so, I began the dating scene. It was probably nowhere I needed to be, but it was the choice I made. I placed an ad on a dating site: Christian female biker seeks like-minded male for companionship.

Within a few days, messages of interest were flooding my inbox. Needless to say, even putting up a Christian ad, the messages that I was receiving were far from appropriate. My emotions were all over the board. Whether I needed to be dating or not was far from my concern. I was lonely and, to be honest, bitter from the pain I had experienced with JD.

The first date I went on was with a guy that had the title of 'Jesus lover' in his ad. My thought was, this guy has got to be ok, he put 'Jesus lover' on his page. I learned quickly that all that glitters is not gold. In conversation, I could tell that his ego was bigger than his muscles and his intention for this site was not Christian related.

He was very handsome and had a nice build and a nice job, but quickly the Holy Spirit began speaking to my heart about how I was not where I was supposed to be. I even caught myself rationalizing with Jesus. "God, he seems nice." I was having a radical debate in my mind.

"Corinna."

"Yes Lord?"

"Do you feel this is where I want you to be?"

I quickly shut my mind and heart down to my communication with the Holy Spirit. I knew inside that I would get answers that I didn't want to hear. I had been hurt and felt I had every right to date. By the time I left from the second date with this guy, I knew I was just as empty as when the date began.

On the way home from the date I could feel the Lord pursuing my heart like never before.

"Corinna, I have big plans for you—bigger than your imagination could ever lay hold to."

I wept and poured my heart out. "Lord, I'm sorry I haven't trusted you and have taken things into my own hands. Forgive me."

From that day on I decided that if a companion was meant for me, they were going to love Jesus more than anything and that would speak for itself.

Some time went by and I had not been on the dating app. I was trusting in the wait. I had taken Mama for a medical procedure, and I would need to drive her. In the family waiting area I received a message: "beautiful eyes." There was no picture with this account and normally I would have deleted the message. For some reason I didn't. This time I wanted to see if he was the right one, at least for companionship. If he was not in this for the right reason, then I would know quickly.

This secret man and I spoke for a few days and exchanged pictures. He asked me on a date and I wanted to be sure this time, so I took things slowly. I wanted this man to know my life story first and the place that God had brought me from. He would either run as fast as he could or he'd embrace it.

We met for breakfast in a local place, this way I could leave and would not be obligated to stay if this thing went sideways. We ate and I began to speak and share the love that Jesus had shown me through all of these years. He shared his testimony as well.

He cried with me when I told him my story. The way he looked at me felt so different than what I had experienced before. I wanted to know more and more of the part of Jesus that lived inside of him. He had a heart for people. I was able to see his kindness to others, and I fell in love with that part of him..

Soon after we started dating, I invited him to church. I was on the prayer team and got to church early. I spoke to one of the greeters at church and told him I had a visitor coming and to please sit him in the area where I would sit.

Of all of the services we had, this service was so powerful! The anointing that morning was so thick and people were getting freed from all sorts of things. The prayer team was face-planted on the Altar seeking the Lord's power and healing. That day the altar was full.

Soon Adam would begin to come regularly with me. We realized together that it was not about the building itself but about building each other in those moments while we were there. We grew stronger every day. He met my kids and quickly began to take time for them. I did the same for his son.

Eleven months later we were married. I invited Adam's ex-wife to the wedding. I had no intention of throwing any stones at her. My only intention was to show her that I was here, not to take her place with my stepson, but to make my own relationship with him and to co-parent alongside her. After I gave my stepson my vows as his "bonus mom," I walked to where his mom was sitting and handed her a yellow rose. I wanted to honor her, to ultimately love her, and to squash anything that the enemy would ever try to place between us.

Adam also gave vows to Jayden. To love her as a "bonus dad," to not take her dad's place, but to also create his own relationship with her. To guide her and nurture her.

What is the cliché? Never say never? When I knew that I was where Jesus wanted me to be, there was nothing to fix or wait for him to change. Adam was hungry for the Father and so was I. We had both come from broken marriages and made many mistakes along the way. I thank God every day for second chances.

CHAPTER FIFTEEN

What Goes Around Comes Around

A few months after our wedding, I received a message from my ex-husband. The message only said a few short words that would pierce my heart deeply:

I. Am. Hungry. Please help us.

Tears streaming down my face, I no longer wanted to keep score or bring up to him the things that had happened. Suddenly, my self-reflection was showing me the time my power had been cut off. It showed me taking baths at night in my son's little kiddie pool in the backyard, water warmed by the sun. I had been in a place where I'd been hurting.

I ran to the next room where Adam was and showed him the message. Compassion fell on us both. My ex-husband and his girlfriend were placing groceries in the snow because they had no power.

Adam and I went and purchased every canned food item we could think of that would not require refrigeration. We went to their house—no longer in need of "he said or she said," only love and food to give. No longer could I think of all the messes that he created or the rebound words reminding him of his past.

The only thing my heart had room for was mercy, for mercy had been shown to me time and time again.

Matthew 25:35-36 says, "For when You saw me hungry, You fed me. When you found me thirsty, you gave me something to drink. When I had no place to stay, you invited me in, and when I was poorly clothed you covered me. When I was sick, you tenderly cared for me, and when I was in prison you visited me." (TPT)

I tried to imagine the lens Jesus saw JD and his girlfriend through. What a beautiful array of kaleidoscope colors He must see. I sincerely wanted better for both of them. Not only free from the chains of addiction, but free from their mind, will, and emotions. I wanted to see them free from the bondage of the world, for it had taken its toll long enough.

I am so thankful that Jesus has been patient with me time and time again. I do not have it all together, but the more I love Him and learn His character, the more I desire to be like His nature.

His compassion and mercy were all I could feel. When I struggled the Lord always sent me someone. I would have never known that he would use Adam and me together to be His hands and feet and receive healing in the process.

CHAPTER SIXTEEN
In Conclusion

I have learned through the years that forgiveness is not for the weak minded. It takes a lot of strength, perseverance, and love to walk the process out. We have to be determined enough to take hold of our thoughts, our pain, and our life and choose forgiveness. When I realized the love that my heavenly Father had for me regardless of what I had done, it allowed me to apply it to others.

Forgiveness does not mean that your pain is insignificant or that you are being disregarded. It is making a decision that you are choosing a life that no longer has control over you. My pain caused me to make terrible decisions, but through it all, God worked for my good even when I could not see it in the present moment.

My prayer through writing this book is that you feel the love of the Father right where you are in life and that you choose to let Him in your heart. When our eyes are open to that love, it covers, it changes, and it heals us in a way that cannot be expressed or measured by any other means. Let Him heal the dark places of your heart that have been buried by anger and frustration.

This book was painful and beautiful to write. Allowing people to look into my life was a hard decision. As you understand and have read in this book, life can be messy and damaging. It took me almost twenty years to get to this point and then a three year writing process. I want to thank my readers for sticking with me through this book as I share my journey. I have no idea what the future will hold for me, but I do know that whatever it brings, Jesus has me in the palm of His hand.

THE END

\#

ACKNOWLEDGEMENTS

First and foremost, I would like to thank God for His continual covering and blessings throughout writing this book. Every moment I have needed someone or something to continue, You have provided and I am forever grateful for Your love, favor and mercy.

To my precious mother, Judy Coalson. For loving me through this journey. For growing with me and for being my prayer partner in everything. For times when I called to share a part of this book and the countless tears fell. You are my rock and without your permission in this I would not be able to share God's miracle of "us".

To my husband Adam, thank you for your encouragement and love. For walking this life out with me and letting Jesus use us together in very special ways. For listening to my testimony that very first day we met. For loving me and my children. For your encouragement to keep writing and to not give up no matter how hard it becomes, I love you.

To my special friend Kristi Widner, for the many hours that you sat with me and helped me with grammar and bringing thoughts together about this book, thank you.

To my confidant Mendie Hawkes, I appreciate you for your concern when I could not come up with a title for my book that I was happy with. You were persistent in helping me, for leaving me a voice memo and giving me the idea for the title to this book. I'm so grateful for you and the life stories that we share, thank you.

A special thank you to my beautiful friend Audrey Lancho. Thank you for editing my book, for your selfless acts of kindness, and pursuit of my story getting out there. I will continue to believe that you are my earth angel. Thank you for helping me make this book the best it could be. May God bless you a thousand fold for your love and dedication to this.

And finally, I want to thank my church family that has allowed me to speak honestly about my story and trusted me with those moments, for loving me unconditionally through the years, and for pushing me to not give up. For always encouraging me to share the love of Christ with others.

ABOUT THE AUTHOR

Corinna Tackett is an ex-convict who served eighteen months in prison. She is now a college graduate and works at her own small business in the salon industry. She speaks to recovering addicts, women's groups, churches, and has served prison ministry teams sharing her message of hope, restoration, and love to local inmates.